NEVER AGAIN

NEVER AGAIN

The Parkland Shooting and the
Teen Activists Leading a Movement

ERIC BRAUN

LERNER PUBLICATIONS ◆ MINNEAPOLIS

Lerner Publications Company
A division of Lerner Publishing Group, Inc.
241 First Avenue North
Minneapolis, MN 55401 USA

For reading levels and more information, look up this title at www.lernerbooks.com.

Image credits: NICHOLAS KAMM/AFP/Getty Images, pp. 2, 10; Kevin Mazur/Getty Images, pp. 6, 16; Jose More/VWPics/UIG/Getty Images, p. 8; Mike Stocker/South Florida Sun-Sentinel/ TNS/Getty Images, p. 9; Formulanone/Wikimedia Commons (CC0 1.0 public domain), p. 13; Emilee McGovern/SOPA Images/LightRocket/Getty Images, pp. 15, 20; Noam Galai/WireImage/ Getty Images, pp. 17, 19; AP Photo/Benjamin Nadler, p. 22; RHONA WISE/AFP/Getty Images, pp. 24, 25, 28; Susan Stocker/Sun Sentinel/TNS/Getty Images, p. 26; Don Juan Moore/Getty Images, p. 27; AP Photo/John Locher, p. 29; Shannon Finney/Getty Images, p. 31; Amy Beth Bennett/Sun Sentinel/TNS/Getty Images, p. 32; Mark Wilson/Getty Images, p. 33; Paul Morigi/ Getty Images, p. 35; Mobilus In Mobili/Flickr (CC BY-SA 2.0), p. 37; Joe Cavaretta/South Florida Sun-Sentinel via AP, p. 38.

Cover: NICHOLAS KAMM/AFP/Getty Images.

Main body text set in Rotis Serif Std 55 Regular 13.5/17. Typeface provided by Adobe Systems.

Library of Congress Cataloging-in-Publication Data

The Cataloging-in-Publication Data for *Never Again: The Parkland Shooting and the Teen Activists Leading a Movement* is on file at the Library of Congress.
ISBN 978-1-5415-5270-8 (lib. bdg.)
ISBN 978-1-5415-5271-5 (eb pdf)

Manufactured in the United States of America
1-45653-41683-9/10/2018

CONTENTS

Marjory Stoneman Douglas High School student Emma González speaks in Washington, DC, on March 24, 2018.

The morning of March 14, 2018, may have started just like any other day. But as soon as the students at Marjory Stoneman Douglas High School in Parkland, Florida, took their seats in class, it felt different. They immediately began to watch the clock. Some may have bounced a leg or tapped a pencil with nervous energy. What was so different about this day? The students at the high school just outside the Florida Everglades were about to launch a major political movement.

One month earlier, the Parkland students had been frantically running through the halls of their school, trying to escape with their lives. A former student armed with an AR-15 rifle had entered the building and shot and killed seventeen Douglas students and staff members. Now the surviving students sat in class and waited for their moment. At 10 a.m., they stood up and walked out.

The halls filled with students, just as they had one month earlier. But this time, the students walked with

Douglas students take part in a walkout to honor the victims of the shooting at their school.

confidence and in an orderly manner. They made their way outside, past reminders of the tragedy: dying flowers, notes, stuffed animals, and other mementos lay in the grass. Some were attached to a chain-link fence. The students kept walking to the football field, joined by reporters and camera crews there to document the moment. They carried signs denouncing gun violence and chanted, "We want change!" A song began to play: "Shine," composed by Douglas students.

Many students were emotional, crying and hugging one another as they left the field and marched 2 miles (3.2 km) to a nearby park. Police had set up barricades to help guide the students. Cars parked along the road, and people honked their support. At the park, students gathered at a memorial that had been set up to honor those who had been killed in the shooting.

One student remarked that they, like other high school students, should be studying for tests. "But," she said, "we face a test of the future."

The students protesting in Parkland were not alone. Students from all around the United States had also left their classrooms at 10 a.m. They, too, carried signs, yelled slogans, and called for lawmakers to focus more attention on gun violence. They walked out in Washington, DC,

Douglas survivors solemnly cross their school's grounds as they protest gun violence.

Students at Georgetown University protested in solidarity with the Douglas activists on March 14, 2018.

and marched to the White House. They walked out in Newtown, Connecticut, the site of another school shooting several years earlier. They walked out in Columbine, Colorado, yet another school shooting locale. From New York to California, students left school in solidarity with the kids in Parkland. In all, nearly one million students across the country left class for the National School Walkout to protest the school-shooting epidemic.

At the heart of this national protest were several Douglas students who had emerged from the tragedy with uplifted voices. Among them, Emma González, Cameron Kasky, Alex Wind, Jaclyn Corin, and David Hogg had been speaking the loudest.

"Every one of these individuals could have died that day," Hogg said, indicating the students protesting in the park. "I could have died that day."

School shootings had happened before, and they were becoming increasingly common. But the US government hadn't taken action to prevent the shootings in the way Hogg and the other students had hoped. So now the students wanted lawmakers to notice that young people were demanding change. They wanted stricter gun laws, including a ban on rifles such as the one the Douglas shooter had used. They wanted their voices heard.

And they were heard. Media outlets worldwide covered the student walkout. News spread quickly about #NeverAgain, the movement begun by the Parkland students. Even lawmakers noticed and made some small changes. But the Parkland students were not done using their voices. They had been heard, and they intended to keep on being heard until schools were safer.

Six Minutes on Valentine's Day

Before Marjory Stoneman Douglas High School became the scene of a mass shooting—and before it became ground zero for a new political movement—it was a fairly typical American high school. Home to about three thousand students from ninth to twelfth grade, Douglas lies in the greater Miami area in southern Florida. It was named after an Everglades environmentalist. Its mascot is the eagle. It has a vegetable garden where science students can run biological tests and where vegetables are grown to be sold on campus. Sometimes, in the campus courtyard, students play musical chairs.

David Hogg was a senior who dreamed of being a broadcast journalist. Emma González, also a senior, was president of the school's gay-straight alliance (GSA) and a team leader on Project Aquila, an experiment that involved launching a weather balloon to learn about collecting weather data. Junior Cameron Kasky was known as a chatty class clown. Another junior, Alex Wind, was a member of the drama club.

Jaclyn Corin was a dancer who planned a career in nursing. On the afternoon of February 14, 2018, Corin made her way to the freshman building on campus to deliver carnations to the freshmen. This was her responsibility on Valentine's Day as junior class president. Shortly after she finished, nineteen-year-old Nikolas Cruz got out of an Uber in front of the school with a large duffel bag. He walked toward the freshman building, entered, and stepped into a stairwell where he thought he wouldn't be seen. There, he pulled a rifle from his duffel.

At 2:21 p.m., freshman Chris McKenna stepped into the stairwell on his way to the restroom, where he ran into Cruz loading his gun. Cruz warned him to leave, and McKenna ran out of the building. Seconds later, the shooting started.

Cruz emerged from the stairwell and fired at a student in the hall, injuring her. He then fired into room 1215,

Marjory Stoneman Douglas High School became a crime scene after former student Nikolas Cruz shot and killed seventeen people there.

killing three. Next, Cruz approached room 1216, where English students were writing in groups. He shot from the doorway, killing one person and wounding three. After that, he moved on to room 1214, where students were learning Holocaust history, and shot six students, killing two of them. Returning to room 1216, Cruz fired again into that room and killed two more students and wounded two others. He killed eleven people on the first floor. As Cruz stormed through the school, the fire alarm went off. Smoke from Cruz's gun may have set off the alarm.

Meanwhile, McKenna had tracked down an adult—assistant football coach Aaron Feis—who went into the building to check on the scene. Feis ran in the direction of the gunfire and shielded students as Cruz shot at them. He died saving those kids.

When Cruz reached the end of the hallway, he went upstairs to the second floor and walked down that hall. But having heard the gunshots, teachers on this floor had covered their windows with paper, turned out the lights, and instructed students to hide. Cruz didn't kill anyone on that floor. On reaching the far end, he again went into the stairwell and climbed to the third floor.

Students on the third floor had likely heard the fire alarm but not the gunshots, so they were trying to exit the building. But they quickly realized what was going on and rushed back into the rooms. Some of the doors were locked, however, and some kids were exposed in the hall. Cruz killed six people on that floor while others scrambled to get away down the stairs. He then went into the third-floor teachers' lounge, shot out some windows, and began shooting at people running away, but he didn't hit anyone from there. At 2:27 Cruz left his rifle in the teachers' lounge and went downstairs, mixing in with the other fleeing kids, and left campus. He had been in the school for six minutes and killed seventeen people, injuring several others.

David Hogg was in his environmental science class when he heard the popping sounds and fire alarm. Because his father was in the FBI and had taught Hogg about weapons, he recognized the popping sounds as gunshots. Still, he thought it was a drill when the alarm went off. He tried to exit the building, but a custodian stopped him and his classmates. He warned them to go back inside. A teacher pulled them into a room, locked

the door, and told them to hide in a closet. Hogg checked social media and learned that the shooting was real—and still going on.

It was hot inside the closet, and some students were crying. Several kids fanned themselves with paper plates. Hogg's younger sister was also a student at the school, so he was worried about her safety. His parents were on his mind as well, and he placed a call to his dad. Many other students also called their parents to tell them that they loved them. And then, though he was scared for his life, Hogg used his phone to interview other students on video.

"As a student journalist, as an aspiring journalist, that's all I could think," he later said. "Get other people's stories on tape. If we all die, the camera survives, and

that's how we get the message out there, about how we want change to be brought about."

Meanwhile, González was locked inside the auditorium. An hour earlier, she had been in her Advanced Placement government class learning about the role of special interest groups in US politics. Corin and Kasky were locked in another classroom together with Kasky's brother, Holden, who has autism, and several other special needs students. Wind, too, had been locked down in a classroom. All the students hid for at least an hour before they got permission to exit. Police and SWAT teams had undertaken a massive sweep of the area, looking for the suspect. By about 2:50, Cruz was at Walmart, buying a soft drink.

Safety for All

Shortly after the shooting at his school, Kasky spoke in a Twitter post about how much he admires his brother, Holden. An online discussion soon followed about the need to keep special needs students safe during a tragedy like the one at Douglas.

Advocates for people with special needs began speaking out about the importance of training law enforcement officers on how to respond to calls involving those with cognitive differences. For example, advocates said that people with autism may not put their hands in the air when asked to by the police. Instead, they may tuck their hands inside a clothing pocket as a way of comforting themselves. Making law enforcement officers aware of such differences may mean the difference between life and death in a crisis.

Cameron Kasky (*above*) and his brother, Holden, have both spoken out since the tragedy at their school.

Holden himself appeared in a video explaining how autistic students may respond differently than other students to a situation with lots of chaos and noise like the one at Douglas. His words served as a powerful advocacy tool for those with disabilities.

An Angry Reaction

Jaclyn Corin was on lockdown for more than two hours, unsure if she would live or die. When a SWAT team finally freed her and she made it home, she did what she often did after school: she went on social media.

Friends were sharing their stories of living through the horrific day. One of her best friends had been killed. Another victim was a freshman girl to whom Corin had given a flower just minutes before Cruz entered the building. "Please pray for my school," Corin posted. Then she posted a call for stricter gun control: "We NEED to work together to bring change."

Cameron Kasky was still in his dad's car after being picked up from school after the shooting when he started posting to Facebook. The first thing he wrote was, "I'm safe." But as the afternoon turned into night, his frustration and anger grew. He, too, began to post about the need for stricter gun control. As he later said, "Our politicians abandoned us by failing to keep guns out of schools. But this time, my classmates and I are going to hold them to account." He had already begun to conceive of a new movement, led by kids that would demand change.

In the classroom where David Hogg was hiding with other students, five SWAT team members burst into the room and ordered everyone to the ground. After surveying the room, the police officers directed the kids to stand, and they walked out of the classroom with their hands still in the air. Once free of the room, many began to run.

Hogg found his dad and sister and learned that one of her friends had been killed. Still, he kept video recording.

Emma González also used her phone to find information about the shooting while she was locked inside the auditorium. That night, finally safe at home, she checked the news again and learned that she knew several students who had been killed. By then Cruz had been found and arrested. The school had expelled him the previous year—and the police had responded to calls at his home thirty-nine times over a period of seven years. Yet in spite of these warning signs, he had easy access to

Members of the Parkland community comfort one another at a vigil honoring the victims.

the semiautomatic gun that killed so many people that day. González thought back to that discussion in class about special interest groups. One of the most influential was one that she strongly opposed: the National Rifle Association (NRA), a powerful gun rights advocacy group whose influence has prevented lawmakers from enacting laws that would make guns harder to obtain. She decided she wanted to speak out publicly about the issue.

The next day, Douglas students attended a vigil to honor those who had been killed in the shooting. Later,

Hogg contacted González with a request: Would she go on air with him in an interview by journalist Anderson Cooper of CNN? González quickly agreed. After the interview, her phone was flooded with texts from people who had seen her on TV. She realized that she had a voice. People were listening.

Kasky said he was in the bathroom at his home and wearing Ghostbusters pajamas when he came up with the idea for the hashtag that would come to define their movement: #NeverAgain. That night, after the vigil, he invited a few friends to his house to talk about what more they could do.

Corin was among those first students to gather with him. The group was small, but in the coming days, it would grow. And Corin had some good news. Congresswoman Debbie Wasserman Schultz, who represents a district outside of Miami, Florida, had seen Corin's Facebook post and wanted to meet her.

A Groundbreaking Speech

National media picked up on the story of the angry, outspoken young activists, and news of their movement began to spread. Online, national groups lined up to take sides. Groups such as Moms Demand Action, which advocate for stronger gun control, voiced strong support for the #NeverAgain teens. Groups such as the NRA expressed their opposition. The discourse was not always

Volunteers with the advocacy group Moms Demand Action hold a banner during a demonstration to lobby the legislature for stricter gun laws.

kind. For example, some who disagreed with the Parkland activists accused David Hogg of being a crisis actor—a professional activist hired to pretend he was a Douglas student.

But the word was getting out. People were paying attention. The Parkland students pressed on with their work. They wanted to draw attention to their concerns about gun policies in the United States.

According to Corin, time was of the essence. If they didn't speak up loudly—and right away—the media would move on to the next story. "The news forgets," she later said. "Very quickly. And if we were all talk and no action, people wouldn't take us as seriously. We needed a critical mass event."

First up was a rally at a federal courthouse in Fort Lauderdale, about 20 miles (32 km) from Parkland. Thousands gathered there with the Parkland students, and several students gave speeches. Among the most noteworthy was a speech by González. Impassioned and angry, González called out lawmakers who offer thoughts and prayers when mass shootings occur but accept money from the NRA and act to block laws that would make people safer from gun violence.

Hogg Takes On His Critics

On February 20, 2018, David Hogg appeared on CNN to address those who accused him of being a paid activist. "I'm not a crisis actor," he told CNN's Anderson Cooper. "I'm someone who had to witness this and live through this, and I continue having to do that."

Some who traditionally supported the NRA spoke up in Hogg's defense. Florida's Republican senator Marco Rubio, for example, defended Hogg in a highly emotional tweet. "Claiming some of the students on tv after #Parkland are actors is the work of a disgusting group of idiots with no sense of decency," he wrote. Gun control advocacy and the issues surrounding it remained an extremely hot-button topic throughout 2018.

Specifically, she pointed out that Congress and President Donald Trump had repealed a law that made it harder for people with certain mental illnesses to buy guns. Senator Chuck Grassley from Iowa, who sponsored the bill, had blamed shootings on the FBI for not doing background checks on mentally ill people. "Well, duh," González said. "You took that opportunity away last year. The people in government who we voted into power are lying to us. And us kids seem to be the only ones who notice."

González speaks at the rally at the Broward County Federal Courthouse in Fort Lauderdale.

Hogg lends his voice to the gun control cause at the Broward County Federal Courthouse.

González criticized those who claim tougher gun laws don't decrease gun violence. She criticized those who claim that more guns would reduce shootings. One by one, González called out what she considered the excuses that have helped sustain a gun culture in the United States, and speaking for a growing movement, she let the world know that those excuses are no longer valid.

González's speech was broadcast nationwide and suddenly made her a household name. All the Parkland activists were becoming celebrities, but they didn't care about fame. They cared about change.

Jaclyn Corin walks with Senator Lauren Book, a supporter of the Parkland students' cause.

And so they moved on to their next event—a meeting with lawmakers at the Florida capitol. The capitol was 450 miles (724 km) away, so there was a lot of planning to do to transport one hundred minors there with chaperones. Florida senator Lauren Book donated her own money for buses to get the kids there and arranged meetings with lawmakers. Corin worked to find housing and food for everyone. As they gathered at a grocery store to get ready for the trip, the press swarmed them. Corin's every move was caught on film. The buses idled nearby, and finally, the students boarded them. At last, they were on the road, with a caravan of media following closely behind.

After an eight-hour bus ride, the group spent the night at Florida State University on cots donated by the Red Cross. At five the next morning, the crew of the TV news show *Good Morning America* came in. Soon after that, the kids were walking to the capitol for their meetings. Small groups of students met with senators and Governor Rick Scott. The students peppered the lawmakers with questions about their positions on gun control. When lawmakers gave answers they liked, the students cheered. In response to answers they didn't like, they groaned.

Overall, the students felt good about their progress. No immediate changes were made, but they hadn't been expecting that. More important was that people were paying attention. The issue of stricter gun laws was now on everybody's radar.

Douglas students and supporters speak out at the Florida capitol.

The Movement Grows

As the weeks went by, the kids appeared on magazine covers, on television, and all over the internet. They became experts at using social media to express their disagreement with the NRA and others who believed that gun laws shouldn't be changed.

Cameron Kasky wrote an opinion article for CNN. Jaclyn Corin wrote one for the magazine *Seventeen*. Through all of this, their message was simple: Lawmakers needed to do more to protect kids from gun violence. If they didn't, the Parkland activists would do all they could to vote those politicians out of office one day.

Even before they returned from the Florida capitol, the young activists had begun to plan the National School Walkout for March 14. Those who appeared on TV news shows also announced another, larger protest: March for Our Lives. That protest would take place in Washington, DC, on March 24—with smaller March for Our Lives protests taking place across the country.

Momentum quickly grew, and a new hashtag began to trend online: #MarchforOurLives. The national gun control organization Everytown for Gun Safety helped the students organize, and many celebrities contributed time and money. George Clooney, Steven Spielberg, and Oprah Winfrey were among the famous names who made large donations. Other wealthy contributors included Justin Bieber, Alyssa Milano, Amy Schumer, St. Vincent, Paul McCartney, Harry Styles, Kanye West, and Kim Kardashian.

The Parkland protesters met regularly at a donated

Kasky rallies a supportive crowd at his high school.

office site near their school to plan their work. They read mail, most of which was supportive but some of which was angry. Some messages included death threats, which the Parkland activists saw as a sign that they were touching a nerve. They launched a website, marchforourlives.com, where they spelled out exactly what they hoped would happen. They wanted laws that would "effectively address the gun violence issues that are rampant in our country." Specifically, they called for

- universal background checks
- equipping the Bureau of Alcohol, Tobacco, Firearms, and Explosives with a digitized, searchable database
- providing the Centers for Disease Control

and Prevention with funding to research the problem of gun violence in America
- banning high-capacity magazines
- banning semiautomatic assault rifles

The group's position was that over the last several years in the United States, mass shootings had almost started to feel commonplace. And although such shootings were still relatively rare, they were increasing. Reflecting further on the #MarchforOurLives mission, Kasky explained that he and his fellow activists wanted to "create a new normal where there's a badge of shame" on politicians who take donations from gun lobbyists.

Students at the Las Vegas Academy of the Arts in Las Vegas, Nevada, were among those who joined in the March 14 protest.

As he put it, "My message for the people in office is: You're either with us or against us. We are losing our lives while the adults are playing around."

The Parkland students became known for their resolute and well-researched message. Yet at the same time, they sometimes brought a touch of humor into their campaign. For example, they nicknamed Florida governor Rick Scott—whose views on gun control tended to stand in opposition to their own—Voldemort, after the main villain in the Harry Potter books. On social media, their serious-but-playful personalities earned them attention, praise, and plenty of followers. Emma González, who was not on Twitter before the shooting, had more followers than the NRA just eleven days after it.

Not only were people paying attention to the Parkland activists. The students' voices were also swaying public opinion. A poll before the shooting showed that about 60 percent of people supported tougher gun laws. That number had grown to about 68 percent after the kids began speaking out. Another poll showed that support for the NRA had dropped to roughly 37 percent.

Even the advertising industry noticed the young activists' message. Some advertisers cut ties with the NRA. And the recreational equipment and athletic apparel store Dick's Sporting Goods stopped selling AR-15s.

Laws slowly started changing too. In Florida, lawmakers passed a new bill that strengthened gun laws. The bill banned bump stocks, a device that can be attached to a semiautomatic rifle to turn it into a fully

Governor Rick Scott of Florida (*right*) eventually departed from his gun-rights stance to sign a bill strengthening gun laws.

automatic one that fires nearly continuously. It also raised the minimum age to buy a weapon and established a waiting period before buyers could get a gun. It gave police the authority to take guns away from people with certain mental health disorders too. Sixty-seven NRA-endorsed Republicans voted for the bill. Governor Rick Scott also broke with his traditional stance on guns by signing the legislation.

March for Our Lives

In the weeks following the shooting at Marjory Stoneman Douglas High School, people around the country had taken cues from the survivors of the shooting. Students had walked out of class to protest gun violence. Citizens had lobbied their lawmakers for gun reform. Tweets, essays, and articles advanced the argument that the

Douglas students were making—that this should never happen again.

That support peaked on March 24, 2018, in Washington, DC. The Douglas students, their friends and families, and about 800,000 supporters marched on Pennsylvania Avenue to protest America's gun policies. Across the United States and around the world, people from about eight hundred other communities marched too, bringing the number of marchers to somewhere between 1.2 and 2 million.

The march in Washington, DC, was the largest protest in decades and one of the largest in history. Crowding

Washington, DC, was a sea of signs on March 24, 2018.

the streets were students, adults, and families with young children. Speakers energized attendees, who clapped especially loudly for Cameron Kasky when he said, "To the leaders, skeptics, and cynics who told us to sit down, stay silent, and wait your turn: Welcome to the revolution." Kasky called for universal background checks on gun sales and a ban on assault rifles.

Kasky went on to read off the names of every student and staff member who was killed in the shooting at Douglas. He took a moment to wish a happy birthday to one of the victims, senior Nicholas Dworet, who wanted to be an Olympic swimmer. He would have turned eighteen that day.

The Parkland students also pointed out that while the shooting at their school had gotten plenty of attention, the public pays far less attention when African American kids are shot. So, striving to make their message more inclusive, the students invited young people of color to speak at the event. Naomi Wadler, an eleven-year-old from Alexandria, Virginia, gave one of the most powerful speeches. "I am here today to acknowledge and represent the African American girls whose stories don't make the front page of every national newspaper," she said.

Also speaking was nine-year-old Yolanda Renee King, the granddaughter of Martin Luther King Jr., who reminded attendees of her grandfather's message. "My grandfather had a dream that his four little children will not be judged by the color of their skin, but by the content of their character," she said to a cheering crowd.

Yolanda Renee King speaks on March 24, 2018, while Jaclyn Corin looks on.

"I have a dream that enough is enough. And that this should be a gun-free world. Period."

One of the main goals of the march was to register people to vote. The Parkland activists believe that real progress can be made only by voting out politicians who oppose more stringent gun laws. Volunteers worked the crowd, carrying clipboards that held voter registration forms. They urged people to not only register to vote but to get seventeen friends to also register—one for each person who was killed inside Douglas High.

When David Hogg took to the podium for his turn to speak, his was one of the most recognizable faces of the movement. He had been particularly present on TV and online, and he'd been singled out by those who opposed his views on guns as a prime target for retaliation.

"Who here is going to vote in the 2018 election?" he asked the crowd. "If you listen real close, you can hear the people in power shaking." He added, "We will not stop until every man, every woman, every child, and every American can live without fear of gun violence."

Six Minutes of Silence

One of the most anticipated speakers of the day was Emma González. Since she'd delivered such a powerful speech at the courthouse in Fort Lauderdale, many people expected that she'd have a lot to say.

But González spoke for less than two minutes. She talked about the effects of gun violence, and she too recited the names of those who had been killed. Then she stood in silence, staring ahead with teary eyes, for more than four uncomfortable minutes. Then a timer went off, and she spoke again.

"Since the time that I came out here, it has been six minutes and twenty seconds," she said. "The shooter has ceased shooting, and will soon abandon his rifle, blend in with the students as they escape, and walk free for an hour before arrest.

"Fight for your lives, before it's someone else's job," she added before leaving the stage.

The march in New York rallied 150,000 participants. Mayor Bill de Blasio noted on Twitter that the public was witnessing a revolution. Many celebrities joined the New

Marchers hold up peace signs in support of Emma González's words.

York protest, including the musician Paul McCartney, who wore a T-shirt that read, "We can end gun violence."

McCartney mentioned to a reporter that one of his best friends had been killed by gun violence near the site of the New York protest, and so the march was particularly important to him. McCartney was referring to John Lennon, who, along with McCartney, had been a member of the musical group the Beatles. Lennon was shot and killed by a gunman outside his New York home in 1980.

Tens of thousands of protesters marched in Parkland, Florida, at a park near the high school where family members and shooting victims spoke. Samantha Mayor, a Parkland junior who had been shot in the knee, marched with a brace on her leg. She was accompanied by her

Samantha Mayor, who was badly injured in the Parkland shooting, lights a memorial candle for victims of violence on Yom HaShoah, or Holocaust Remembrance Day.

mom. Parkland student Adam Buchwald gave a speech, stoking the crowd for a long fight against gun violence. "The finish line at the end of the march here today in Parkland . . . is our beginning line," he said. "We are just getting started!"

In some communities, gun rights activists staged their own, smaller rallies. Their message was that the Second Amendment to the US Constitution guarantees the right to bear arms without restriction and that any attempt to curtail that right was unconstitutional. But the prevailing message on March 24 was that of March for Our Lives: that new gun laws can and should be enacted to protect people—and that such laws could be enacted without infringing on anyone's constitutional rights.

Leading into the Future

The March for Our Lives did not create change right away. The Parkland kids knew it would be a long road, and they'd been prepared for that. For them, the priority was getting young people registered to vote—and then getting them to show up at the polls once voting day rolled around.

It wouldn't be easy. Only 39 percent of voters between the ages of eighteen and twenty voted in the 2016 election, and getting voters to come out for midterm elections is even harder. Only 14 percent of young voters voted in the 2014 midterms.

Still, the Parkland teens have permanently changed the discussion about gun violence. Their impact is deep and undeniable. And they have even higher ambitions. They have talked about holding a March for Our Lives every year on March 24. They have talked about expanding their campaign to other issues, such as climate change and net neutrality. And in June 2018, they announced a fifty-city bus tour to register voters.

No matter what happens, these battle-scarred teenagers have inspired other young people to pay attention, be aware, and get involved. They have inspired the leaders of tomorrow. And many of them are likely to *be* the leaders of tomorrow. They have already reshaped the politics of the future. As Parkland student Autumn McKinney said, Nikolas Cruz could never have imagined the unintended impact his actions had. "Even though he did something terrible, it started something amazing," she said. "He didn't win."

IMPORTANT DATES

February 14, 2018   Gunman Nikolas Cruz kills seventeen and injures many more in a shooting at Marjory Stoneman Douglas High School in Parkland, Florida.

February 15   A vigil honors those who were killed.

February 17   A gun control rally takes place at the Broward County Federal Courthouse. Emma González gives an impassioned speech.

February 21   Douglas students travel to the state capitol in Tallahassee to speak, meet with lawmakers, and demand gun reform.

February 28   Dick's Sporting Goods announces it will no longer sell AR-15s.

March 14   Students from around the United States walk out of class to show solidarity with Douglas students.

March 24   March for Our Lives events around the world protest gun violence.

June 3	Hogg, González, and other seniors graduate from Marjory Stoneman Douglas High.
June 4	The Parkland teens announce a two-month bus tour across the country to hold voter registration drives in fifty cities.

SOURCE NOTES

8   Kristyn Wellesley, "Parkland High School Students Walkout, March to Memorial Set Up for 17 Shooting Victims," *USA Today,* March 14, 2018, https://www.usatoday.com/story/news/nation-now/2018/03/14/parkland-high-school-students-walkout-march-memorial-set-up-17-shooting-victims/423975002/.

9   Phillip Valys, Anne Geggis, and Aric Chokey, "National Walkout Day: Students from Stoneman Douglas and across U.S. Call for Safety, Gun Control," *Fort Lauderdale (FL) Sun Sentinel,* March 14, 2018, http://www.sun-sentinel.com/local/broward/parkland/florida-school-shooting/fl-florida-school-shooting-walkouts-20180314-story.html.

11   Valys, Geggis, and Chokey.

15–16 Ilene Prusher, "A Student Started Filming during the Florida School Shooting. He Hasn't Stopped," *Time,* February 15, 2018, http://time.com/5161034/florida-school-shooting-survivor/.

18   Dave Cullen, "'The News Forgets Very Quickly': Inside the Marjory Stoneman Douglas Students' Incredible Race to Make History," *Vanity Fair,* March 7, 2018, https://www.vanityfair.com/news/2018/03/inside-the-marjory-stoneman-douglas-students-race-to-make-history.

18   Betsey Guzior, "Social Media Savvy Students Drive Discussion on Gun Control," Bizwomen, accessed July 24, 2018, https://www.bizjournals.com/bizwomen/news/latest-news/2018/02/social-media-savvy-students-drive-discussion-on.html?page=all.

18   Cameron Kasky, "Parkland Student: My Generation Won't Stand for This," *CNN,* February 20, 2018, https://www.cnn.com/2018/02/15/opinions/florida-shooting-no-more-opinion-kasky/index.html.

23   Nicole Chavez, "School Shooting Survivor Knocks Down 'Crisis Actor' Claim," *CNN,* February 21, 2018, https://www.cnn.com/2018 /02/21/us/david-hogg-conspiracy-theories-response/index.html.

23   Chavez.

23   Cullen, "News Forgets."

24   CNN staff, "Florida Student Emma Gonzalez to Lawmakers and Gun Advocates: 'We Call BS,'" *CNN,* February 17, 2018, https://www.cnn.com/2018/02/17/us/florida-student-emma -gonzalez-speech/index.html.

29   "Mission Statement," March for Our Lives, accessed July 24, 2018, https://marchforourlives.com/mission-statement/.

30   Quinn Scanlan, "Florida Teen Shooting Survivors Announce 'March for Our Lives' Demonstration in Washington," *ABC News,* February 18, 2018, https://abcnews.go.com/Politics/florida -teen-shooting-survivors-announce-march-washington-demand /story?id=53178265.

31   Jennifer Calfas, "The Teens Who Survived the Florida School Shooting Are Organizing a National March to Demand Gun Control," *Time,* February 18, 2018, http://time.com/5164939 /march-for-our-lives-florida-shooting/.

34   Joe Heim, "Student Leader Says Legislators Will Be Voted Out of Office," *Washington Post,* March 24, 2018, https://www .washingtonpost.com/local/2018/live-updates/politics/march -for-our-lives/student-leader-says-legislators-will-be-voted -out-of-office/?utm_term=.240e927a8f94.

34   Katie Reilly, "Emma González's Stunning Silence for Parkland: The Latest on March for Our Lives," *Time,* March 24, 2018, http://time.com/5213929/march-for-our-lives-live-updates/.

34–35   Reilly.

36   "March for Our Lives Highlights: Students Protesting Guns Say 'Enough Is Enough,'" *New York Times,* March 24, 2018, https://www.nytimes.com/2018/03/24/us/march-for-our-lives .html.

36   James Loke Hale, "The Transcript of David Hogg's March for Our Lives Speech Will Bring Tears to Your Eyes," Bustle, March 24, 2018, https://www.bustle.com/p/the-transcript-of-david-hoggs -march-for-our-lives-speech-will-bring-tears-to-your-eyes -8596305.

36   "March for Our Lives," *New York Times.*

37   "March for Our Lives."

38   Reilly, "Emma González's Silence."

39   Reilly.

SELECTED BIBLIOGRAPHY

Alter, Charlotte. "The School Shooting Generation Has Had Enough." *Time,* March 22, 2018. http://time.com/longform/never-again -movement/.

Andone, Dakin. "Student Journalist Interviewed Classmates as Shooter Walked Parkland School Halls." *CNN,* February 18, 2018. https://www.cnn.com/2018/02/17/us/david-hogg-profile-florida -shooting/index.html.

Cooper, Kelly-Leigh. "In Florida Aftermath, US Students Say 'Never Again.'" *BBC,* February 18, 2018. https://www.bbc.com/news/world -us-canada-43105699.

Cullen, Dave. "'The News Forgets. Very Quickly': Inside the Marjory Stoneman Douglas Students' Incredible Race to Make History." *Vanity Fair,* March 7, 2018. https://www.vanityfair.com/news/2018 /03/inside-the-marjory-stoneman-douglas-students-race-to-make -history.

Hobbs, Stephen, Yiran Zhu, and Aric Chokey. "New Details: How the Parkland School Shooting Unfolded." *Fort Lauderdale (FL) Sun Sentinel,* April 24, 2018. http://www.sun-sentinel.com/local/broward /parkland/florida-school-shooting/sfl-florida-school-shooting -timeline-20180424-htmlstory.html.

"March for Our Lives Highlights: Students Protesting Guns Say 'Enough Is Enough.'" *New York Times,* March 24, 2018. https://www.nytimes .com/2018/03/24/us/march-for-our-lives.html.

Reilly, Katie. "Emma González's Stunning Silence for Parkland: The Latest on March for Our Lives." *Time,* March 24, 2018. http://time .com/5213929/march-for-our-lives-live-updates/.

Valys, Phillip, Anne Geggis, and Aric Chokey. "National Walkout Day: Students from Stoneman Douglas and across U.S. Call for Safety, Gun Control." *Fort Lauderdale (FL) Sun Sentinel,* March 14, 2018. http://www.sun-sentinel.com/local/broward/parkland/florida-school -shooting/fl-florida-school-shooting-walkouts-20180314-story.html.

Witt, Emily. "How the Survivors of Parkland Began the Never Again Movement." *New Yorker,* February 19, 2018. https://www.newyorker .com/news/news-desk/how-the-survivors-of-parkland-began-the -never-again-movement.

FURTHER READING

BOOKS

Braun, Eric. *Taking Action for Civil and Political Rights*. Minneapolis: Lerner Publications, 2017. Read about other inspiring activists in this book.

Otfinoski, Steven. *Gun Control*. New York: Children's Press, 2014. Learn more about an issue that took the country by storm in the wake of the Parkland shooting.

Thompson, Laurie Ann. *Be a Changemaker: How to Start Something That Matters*. New York: Simon Pulse, 2014. Learn how to make a difference just as the Parkland activists are doing.

WEBSITES

Everytown for Gun Safety
https://everytown.org
Find out more about Everytown for Gun Safety, an organization against gun violence.

March for Our Lives
https://marchforourlives.com
Read about the movement started by the Parkland activists.

Moms Demand Action for Gun Sense in America
https://momsdemandaction.org
Moms Demand Action is a gun safety advocacy group. You can learn more at their website.

INDEX